WORK-FROM-HOME BUSINESS IDEAS

ANTHONY EKANEM

Copyright © Anthony Ekanem
All Rights Reserved.

ISBN 978-1-68509-310-5

This book has been published with all efforts taken to make the material error-free after the consent of the author. However, the author and the publisher do not assume and hereby disclaim any liability to any party for any loss, damage, or disruption caused by errors or omissions, whether such errors or omissions result from negligence, accident, or any other cause.

While every effort has been made to avoid any mistake or omission, this publication is being sold on the condition and understanding that neither the author nor the publishers or printers would be liable in any manner to any person by reason of any mistake or omission in this publication or for any action taken or omitted to be taken or advice rendered or accepted on the basis of this work. For any defect in printing or binding the publishers will be liable only to replace the defective copy by another copy of this work then available.

Contents

Preface — v

1. Information-related Businesses — 1
2. Service-related Businesses — 8
3. Fitness, Beauty And Health-related Businesses — 13

Conclusion — 19

Preface

If you are one of the countless people who are struggling to find a good-paying office job or perhaps one of those who prefer working in the comfort of their homes, there are a lot of options that you could choose from. Working a home-based job is not half bad. Although there are perks when it comes to working an actual job in an office, working from home comes with its upsides as well. There are a lot of home-based business opportunities for everyone. With the help of the internet, friends, and a lot of perseverance, you could turn a handful of budgets into a thriving business. When it comes to starting your home-based business, there are a lot of things you need to consider.

THE BUDGET

First, there is the budget. Setting up a business always starts with a budget – the amount of money you can raise for the business. Well, of course, you do need to have some motivation or an idea of what your business is going to be like. But again, it boils down to how much money you can shell out to start. Let us say you have got limited resources and got little to spare. It is not a problem once you get your finances straight. After that, it is all about getting there, having your business kick-started, and working hard.

SKILLS AND ABILITIES

Once you have gotten your finances ready, the next thing you want to do is look at your skills and abilities. What are you good at? Most of the time, you could make a business out of the things that you have expert skills in. Baking is a good example of a skill that you can make a business of in the comfort of your home. Though it may seem like a cliché and like everybody has been there, done that, but there is still a good chance of making a large sum out of baking. It requires less money to start, and you could easily back out if you do not feel like it is going anywhere without spending too much. This is just one of the many examples of home businesses that you could make by utilizing your skills.

THE TARGET MARKET

When putting up a business, you must always think of your target market. It is an essential aspect when running any business. Since you are going to be conducting business at home, you must thoroughly evaluate the bounds of your business. Think of the people who are going to be your customers and you can start from there. Once you acquire your target market, all that is left for you to do is make sure that your business runs smoothly and that your products and services are of the highest quality.

This book will introduce you to some of the most realistic and creative ideas on how you can start your business at home with a minimal budget. Read on, be inspired, and start your home business today.

CHAPTER ONE

Information-Related Businesses

1. **ONLINE VENDING**

Now, it is not surprising to hear about people buying stuff over the internet. It is booming businesses, and companies are making a lot of money out of it, and so can you. It is easy, it requires the least start-up capital, and it does not take much of your time. You could make your website and sell your products from there. Or perhaps you could use one of those classified ad websites that will make it easier for you to sell your products.

Here are some helpful ideas on how you can start up an online selling business at home:

i. **Picking the Right Product**

An essential piece of online selling is the product. What goods or services do you think will sell like hot cake? The number of choices can be overwhelming, so you need to sit down and think things over. Choose a product that sells quickly. Something that people need. Selling gadgets and other non-essential items can be the right choice, but these products tend to sell over a lengthy period. This is not something you would want to happen, especially if you are on a short budget.

ii. Choose Your Target Market

The buying public is made up of different age groups. Your product must be able to suffice the needs of at least one age group to have a higher ROI (Return on Investment). Beauty products, for instance, are more flexible. You can sell them to young people and people of mature age. It is this principle that will make your investment worth it. The bigger your audience is, the better sales are for you. Again, you are going to be selling your products online, so this means a lot of people could access what you are selling, which makes it easier compared to manually giving away adverts like flyers and pamphlets.

iii. Go Social!

Probably the best way to sell your product today is through the help of social media. With tons of users logging in every single day, it is not that hard to get your brand and product noticed. It is free, easy to use, and helps a lot in terms of advertisement and sales. All you need to do is to create a profile page for your product, include all the bits and pieces of information that you could put in, and start spreading the word. Start by linking your product page with your friends, build a fan base, add more friends, and share the links to your product. This will make it easier for people to notice your brand and product and will help you make a business as you work in the comfort of your own home.

iv. **Gaining Credibility**

When it comes to selling products online, there is no better way of gaining credibility than to have user reviews and testimonials. It is these user comments that mean the most for your product. This will add legitimacy to your brand since new customers would have a basis for buying your product. If you have got good reviews, the better it is for your product, and more people will be interested in purchasing from you.

2. WEB DEVELOPER/WEBSITE CREATION

Back then, developing websites were left to people who had extended hours and intense programming courses. However, today, web development can be done by almost anyone who has access to a fully functional computer and fast internet connection. If you are a novice in this field, you could still make a business out of it. You could learn how to develop a website through online courses and tutorials. And of course, you need to have important accreditation, especially when you start your web development business. The next thing you need to keep in mind is the competition. You must be able to network your skills over the internet extensively. Finding customers these days can be hard but still doable given adequate persistence and knowledge.

Prospect Clients:

There is a lot of fish in the sea. There will always be people and businesses that need a website. Start by scouting the people you know. Most of them might not need one now, but at least you are spreading the word. Your next stop will be the local establishments and businesses in your neighbourhood. If it is a small establishment, it is most likely that they do not have a website yet. Again, it all boils down on how you are going to market your business. There is a lot of competition, and you need to have an advantage over them, like providing better offers to your clients and providing excellent after-sales services.

Being a web developer at home will not cost you much money but will require you to spend a lot of your hours in front of your computer learning new codes. It is a fun job if you think of it. It is not too hard to get your business running. All that is important is gaining the skills necessary for the business and finding the clients.

3. BLOGGING

A blog is a shortened term for "Weblog". It is a website that contains entries like articles and other content. A blog is relatively easy to do. There are more than 20 million blogs out on the internet, and there are tons of new ones coming out each day. It is so easy that you could make a blog in less than 15 minutes. If you are going down the road of blogging, you must ask yourself and understand the following:

How Can I Make Money Out of A blog?

This is a pretty good question. How will you earn with a blog? Well, AdSense, that is. Once your blog attracts a lot of visitors each day, you could enrol your blog into Google's AdSense. This will place ads on your blog, which will enable you to earn money. If a lot of people click on the advertising on your blog or just simply by visiting, you could earn money. It is not that much, but accumulated visits and ad clicks can earn you enough money. Apart from that, you can also sell some products or services if you have any. It is a matter of marketing once you get your audience lined up.

How Much Will A Blog Cost Me?

Creating a blog could be free. There are many blogging platforms on the internet that allows you to create a blog for free. Of course, free always mean limited. Although you could still have your blog up and running, it does not have an absolute uniqueness and the ability to customize every single layout fully. Blogging platforms usually offer hosting services and domain names for a reasonable price. This means you could make a blog that has got a unique domain name and can only cost you roughly $50 to $100 a year. That is a reasonable price to start.

4. FREELANCE WRITING

Do you have a passion for writing and have a way with words? It is easy to make a business out of writing. There is a lot of options to choose from. You could write content for a website, write eBooks, magazines, and much more. It is a profitable business, takes little expense and you could write probably anywhere you like as long as you have an internet connection and a computer with you.

How Can I Earn Through Writing?

Think about the possibilities. There is a lot of businesses near your area, and all of them need quality content. The question is not about why they are going to need to hire a writer but rather what they will get when they do. If your target market is your local businesses near you, then you should prepare an excellent proposal. Most of the businesses would turn your services down but let them know about the good stuff that is in it for them, and they will surely reconsider. You could also earn through writing online. There are a lot of people and companies that need superstar writers. Once you have a nice-looking portfolio, it is easy to attract clients all over.

Online Freelance Writing

The internet has a lot to offer for freelance writers. Freelancing websites often show a lot of client job offers that need to be filled in. Your skillset allows you to gain bigger offers as you progress. You could stick to fulltime employment, or you could choose to do contract-based projects. As you progress, you will probably face a lot of different writing styles, different types of articles, and a lot of employers. Just bear in mind that you are writing as a passion and not just for a job. Though your main aim is to do writing as a business but doing it passionately is somewhat more productive, and the results are always good.

5. SOCIAL MEDIA MARKETING

Millions of people across the world are using social media. It is an inexpensive form of entertainment that everybody can enjoy. It is where people socialise. It is where people share their lives with people they know. Conversely, apart from being a form of entertainment, social media has become a marketing haven. Millions of businesses have been harnessing social media as an effective means for marketing their brand and product. Sadly, not everyone is familiar with how marketing works with social media. Now, that is where the fun part begins and an opportunity for you.

What Is Social Media Marketing?

Social Media Marketing is a variant of internet marketing that is aimed at reaching a branding or product goal. This always involves the use of contents, images, and videos on different social media platforms. Its primary goal is to spread brand awareness. Since real people are using social media, the likelihood of gaining live visits from prospect customers are higher compared to other means.

How to Become A Social Media Expert

It takes time to become familiar with how everything works. There are a lot of aspects to investigate, and each time social media platforms launch an update, there are changes that you also need to investigate. Therefore, what you must do is to find an online course on social media marketing and study very hard. It is not much to ask since you are just staying at your home with the least expenses, of course. And just like any other skill-based information related job, you will grow as time progresses.

There is no unlearning or forgetting what you have learned. Once you get to the point of becoming familiar with the process, all that is left is to go up. It is a good-paying business, does not take a toll on your budget, and, finally, gives you more knowledge to grow in the industry.

CHAPTER TWO

Service-Related Businesses

1. FOOD DELIVERY SERVICE

This type of business is quite effective if you are located near offices and establishments filled with workers. Remember, not everyone has the luxury of going out for lunch just to grab a bite. Start by scouting several offices in your location. Make inquiries around and offer your services to people within the vicinity. It will be hard at first, especially if you do not know anybody in that location. Be friendly and talk to anyone. This is how it all starts. Word of mouth can later serve as a good advert about your goods or services.

If you can manage, try to bring along some samples with you. This will pretty much give the people there what you are offering, how much it costs, and how good it is. This often comes with a lot of persuasions. However, you would not need it that much if the clients are satisfied. They will come looking for you the next time around.

Check for any competitors and see what they are offering. This will give you an advantage over your competition for some time. On the other hand, if the other party is smart enough, they will soon catch up with a better offer to entice your clients to switch to them. Just prepare a countermeasure. Do promos or add on a few extra. It will not hurt your budget. Although it might cost you a bit, it is worth more than what you will earn.

Let Your Brand Be Known!

Once people get to know you and your services, all you need to do is to set a high-level standard for the food and your delivery. It is the taste and on-time delivery that counts. Whatever you do, never be late. An empty stomach often cooks up an angry mind, and a hungry and angry person is not what you would want to deal with. Not only will you lose a customer, but it will cost you your reputation as well.

The Handyman Service

If you are pretty much a know-it-all kind of person when it comes to fixing things, you could very well make it a nice business. There are a lot of homes that need a helping hand occasionally. However, this job is not for everyone. It takes a lot of skills and know-how to do some repairs. People who do this kind of job are not afraid to face doing odd jobs like fixing a ceiling, fixing stuff down the basement, and just about anything that needs repairing.

Of course, at first, you may need to have a handyman certification. Everyone who would want to have something repaired would want it done by a certified professional. Start locally. You could start fixing your neighbour's broken stuff for a fee. You could do all these to create a portfolio for yourself.

Getting a Franchise

Some companies that offer handyman services are open for franchising. If you have extra cash to spare, you can get a franchise and get going. Although this is a bit of the expensive route rather than running on a tight budget. However, this option gives you the advantage of its branding. Given that the company already has an outstanding background, all you need to do is uphold the quality of service, and you are good to go.

2. LANDSCAPING/LAWN CARE

Remember children coming over to your home and offering to mow your lawn for a fee? This is the adult version of it. If you are good at landscaping, gardening, or perhaps you like a more physical job, this is it!

Landscaping and lawn care is doing the dirty work to transform a bare lawn into a beautiful, well-maintained garden. You can offer this type of service throughout the neighbourhood. You can take pictures of your finished work, put it in a photo album, and show them to your prospective clients.

It is a fun job! The more artistic you are, the better the results will be. Your prospect market should first be your neighbourhood. This way, you would have fewer problems looking for clients. Other than that, there would not be an issue with credibility since they already know who you are and how refined your work is.

Although this may not be the most profitable business out there, it sure is fulfilling. Think about this, you have got 30 houses in your neighbourhood, and all of them got lawns. Just imagine that each one of them would need to have their gardens maintained. You would have a client for each day of the month. It is not that much of a hassle, gives you a lot of exercises, gives you enough money, and you could enjoy what you are doing.

3. TUTORING SERVICES

If you have the knack for teaching, this one is undoubtedly for you. Surely a lot is going on the internet that would make tutoring services a second option. However, for some people, tutoring services are a lot easier. The learning process is a lot faster. Teaching is, of course, a lot better if someone is there with you while you study. If you are good at relaying information to other people, this is specially made for you. However, you might need to get a certification before you could practice tutoring at a broader scope. But if you are simply starting up, you could always begin with a few students starting with your neighbours perhaps.

How Well Will Tutoring Pay Me?

It is all up to you. If your services are quite profound, you could charge a decent fee, but if you are still priming yourself, you should not yet put your hopes up of getting paid well enough. Well, it is all about practice and dedication, just like how your teachers did when you were still in school. It is a matter of knowing how to handle people and convey learning as if you were just having a casual conversation. You could also expand and tutor people online. There are a lot of websites and people who need tutoring.

4. TRANSLATOR/LANGUAGE TUTOR

Do you speak many tongues? If yes, this is one that is worth your while. It is no surprise to see people from different countries trying to learn the local language. Being multilingual is not something that everyone could do. It is an acquired talent that not all people possess. Other than being useful, you could use this multiple language fluency to your advantage. Many people are looking for persons that can teach them a new language. And the job pays well.

The best thing about this is that you could work from home without the need to go elsewhere: just a computer, stable internet connection, and the ability to speak fluently different languages. Working from home as a translator for a foreign company is one thing that will land you an excellent pay. A lot of companies are always in search of people who are fluent in different languages. These people are essential, especially when companies decide with foreign clients.

Well, of course, you do need to become familiar with different languages first before you could become a translator. Not just word for word translation but the local dialect as well. Companies would gladly pay anyone good at translating.

CHAPTER THREE

Fitness, Beauty and Health-Related Businesses

You will be surprised to find out that there is a lot about beauty and wellness that you could do a business of simply at home. There are plenty to choose from, whichever suits your skills, personality, and passion. This kind of job usually requires a prerequisite, which is the eagerness to achieve and share beauty and wellness for everyone. Not only are you imparting your skills and passion, but you are also sharing that fulfilling experience of looking and being healthy and beautiful.

1. **YOGA INSTRUCTOR**

Yoga is a practice of self-discipline, or being able to control one's physical body, achieving a calm and relaxed state of mind. Being a yoga instructor can be made a home business that you will surely like. Most people nowadays are too stressed with work, frustrated, and tired. The sad part is that not everyone could easily overcome the problems that life has to offer. The good part is when you come in. As a yoga instructor, you are not just teaching people to control their bodies but also teach them how to ease their minds. You can make very good money from this business. If you are hesitant about going down this path, think about how you could help people. This is more of turning passion into a business and one that helps others.

Stress Relief

A difficult workweek can do so much for an individual, let alone perform the same job over and over for years. It puts a toll on anyone, which is why most people turn to yoga. With yoga, you can learn how to control your breathing, meditate, and relax. It is a common sight to see people going out occasionally for a drink to unwind and relieve all the stress. But does the stress go away after you have bathed yourself in alcohol? The answer is no, and most likely, you will earn yourself a nasty headache. You can be that person that will bring about a change in the people and help them unwind and learn to relax in a less harmful way. Self-discipline has always been the best way to control one's stress. If you are already an expert at meditating and know yoga, you can quickly turn your knowledge and experience into a business.

2. HOME BEAUTICIAN

This home business aims to bring out the beauty of anyone. Why engage in this kind of business? First, this business is based on your skills. This means the more skilful you are at doing makeup, getting nails done, and anything related to beautification, the more competent you are to become a home-based beautician. You do not need a degree of any sort to become a beautician. Many online courses teach the basics and the more advanced methods of making anyone beautiful. This, of course, is not limited to makeup application or manicure and pedicure. This is a wide-ranging kind of gig that can include hair removal, body piercing, foot and hand massage, and so many more.

Will I Prosper in This Kind of Business?

There is a lot of money in this kind of business since everyone at some point would want to have their hair, nails, skin, and just about any part of their body done. The idea is first to learn how things are done, what equipment you should be using, and being familiar with this kind of industry. There are a lot of makeup artists that have become famous in their profession, and so can you. Learning is an easy task, but the actual work can be a challenge for those who are untrained.

How Much Will It Cost Me?

If you are going to focus on being a makeup artist, you may need to shell out a bit of cash for the equipment. However, unlike any other type of business, your equipment does not get broken or would require upkeep. Makeup does not run out fast, and you would already have a lot of applications before you could use up a whole kit.

3. PERSONAL FITNESS TRAINER

Let us face it, and there are a lot of people who need help. The kind of support that ends up being physically fit and healthy. Have you ever encountered a fitness trainer before? It is easy to know why people hire them in, to begin with. These people are physically fit, and they have their bodies to show that. No questions were asked. You should be one too! If you want to pursue this kind of business, you must first invest in yourself. There is no product here that could help you out that much but simply yourself. Fitness instructors are skilful in the field of bodily fitness.

This business can be a high paying one if you know how to pick your clients. Although it is not all the time that you could encounter a good tipper, you will meet one now and then. Apart from being a fun business, this also allows you to stay healthy yourself. Just remember, being a personal instructor is somewhat an inspiration, a role model that your clients can look up to. You do not need to invest a lot of money in becoming a fitness trainer but rather a lot of your time. But if you are stuck at home with nothing else to do but spent your time, this will be the perfect opportunity for you.

4. MASSAGE THERAPIST

If you want to become a massage therapist, you must first acquire some certification. Health regulations usually require this if in case you run into some problems with your clients. A home-based massage therapist is a nice business to start, especially if you are familiar with this field. You could start-up within your home, letting your clients enjoy a relaxing massage. This will cut costs down drastically. Just be sure that you do make a room in your house that is suited for this business. You may need to invest in a massage table that is specially designed to be used for massage sessions. Oil and other vital items like perfumed candles are also part of your expenditures.

If you are planning on putting up a small massage business within your home, it is best to have someone to assist you. Train someone that you know who is willing to do the job. Later, more and more clients will pour in depending on the quality of services you offer.

5. BEAUTY ADVISER

Most people face problems with their looks, their style, and choice of clothing. It is a typical situation for any woman to encounter hours and hours picking clothes in the closet only to end up not picking anything. You can harness this indecisiveness as an opportunity for you to put up your own beauty adviser business. You could tell people what and what not to wear, how they style themselves, and how to look gorgeous. Of course, you need to have an in-depth understanding of how the fashion world works and how you could apply it to your business. Be creative, embrace the trend, and stand out. It is a matter of creativity that this kind of business will prosper.

Conclusion

Staying at home does not mean that you cannot earn money. There are a lot of opportunities to make good money all within the comfort of your own home. With the availability of the internet, there are many things you can do to earn money. There is at least one type of business that is suitable for each person. All that is required is the following:

Creativity and Ingenuity

When it comes to building a business, it always starts small. It is advisable to start with minimal capital, so when in the worst case it fails, you will not fall that hard. Also, even if you start small, you must always dream big, be creative, plan ingenious methods on how you could expand your business and prosper. Many successful entrepreneurs have started their business in their garage or their backyard and made it big-time. In any business, what is needed is the capacity to be creative. Explore unexplored areas and formulate unique ideas and put them into action.

The Capital

Let us face it. These days' it is hard to start a business without any capital. Before you jump right into a business, you must evaluate your financial capacity. Ask yourself how much can you spare? How much money can you acquire? These are just some of the many questions that are involved in raising capital for your business. In advance, plan the things you would like to do.

Perseverance, Passion, and Will

These are the most important factors of all. Setting up a business entails a willingness to take risks. Passion is also necessary. Businesses built with passion often succeed,

CONCLUSION

especially if the entrepreneur who founded it has the will to carry on whatever the circumstances may be.

There is nothing that could stand in your way in terms of building a business but yourself. Assess your skills, continue to learn and grow, and become what you want to be. Do what makes you happy.

www.ingramcontent.com/pod-product-compliance
Lightning Source LLC
Chambersburg PA
CBHW070846220526
45466CB00002B/905